THIS JOURNAL BELONGS TO

_____

...ONLY THE CAT IS POETRY.

- FRENCH PROVERB

WAY DOWN DEEP, WE'RE ALL
MOTIVATED BY THE SAME URGES.

CATS HAVE THE COURAGE
TO LIVE BY THEM.

- JIM DAVIS

THERE ARE FEW THINGS IN LIFE

MORE HEARTWARMING

THAN TO BE

WELCOMED BY A CAT.

-TAY HOHOFF

IN ANCIENT TIMES CATS WERE

WORSHIPPED AS GODS.

THEY HAVE NEVER FORGOTTEN THIS.

-TERRY PRATCHETT

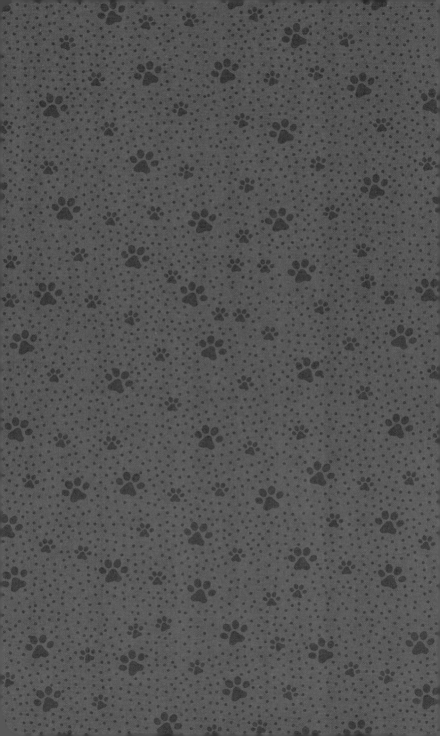

THE SMALLEST FELINE

IS A MASTERPIECE.

-LEONARDO DA VINCI

THERE ARE MANY

INTELLIGENT SPECIES

IN THE UNIVERSE, THEY ARE ALL

OWNED BY CATS.

-UNKNOWN

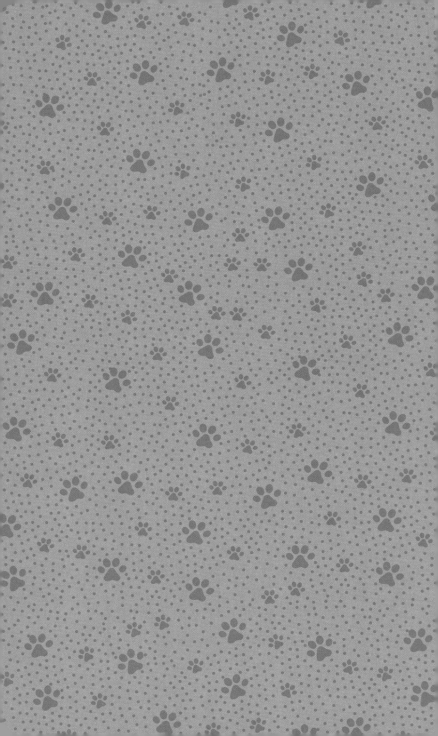

...THE ONLY IDENTIFICATION THAT COULD

TRUTHFULLY BE INSCRIBED

ON ANY CAT'S COLLAR WOULD BE,

"THIS IS THE CAT'S CAT."

-ELMER HOLMES DAVIS

A CAT IS THERE

WHEN YOU CALL HER—IF SHE DOESN'T HAVE

SOMETHING BETTER TO DO.

-BILL ADLER

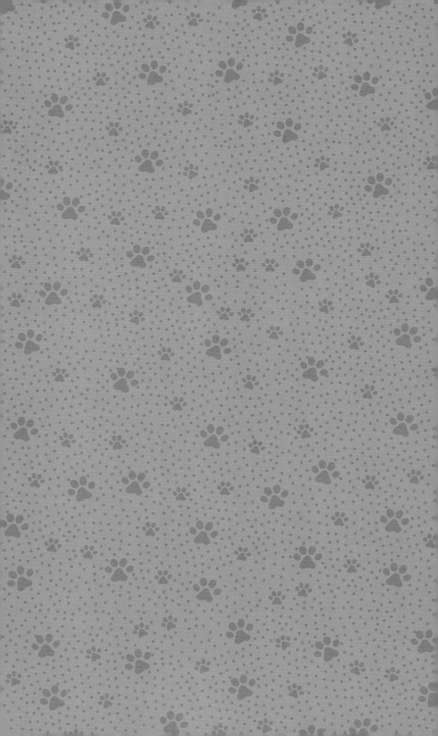